Original title:
Laughing Through the Quest for Meaning

Copyright © 2025 Creative Arts Management OÜ
All rights reserved.

Author: Elliot Harrison
ISBN HARDBACK: 978-1-80566-250-1
ISBN PAPERBACK: 978-1-80566-545-8

The Playful Pilgrim's Pursuit

With a hop and a skip, I start my way,
Each stumble a giggle, come what may.
The map in my hand, all upside down,
I'm lost but I dance, a joyful clown.

The sun teases clouds in a bright blue sky,
I wave to the birds, they pass me by.
With pockets of laughter and shoes full of glee,
I trip on my dreams, then smile at the spree.

A talking tree ticks off its own list,
I ask for wisdom, it just lets out a missed,
Chuckle like whispers of secrets so old,
Each giggle a story, each leaf a bold gold.

At the end of the road, I find my fate,
A mirror reflecting my own funny state.
The lesson's a riddle, wrapped up in jest,
Embracing the wild is truly the best.

Chuckles and Chances under the Cosmic Vault

Stars wink at me, twinkling in jest,
They tickle my thoughts, put luck to the test.
A comet zooms by, with a wink and a grin,
I dive into laughter, I'm ready to spin.

With each cosmic sigh, the planets align,
I trip over stardust, it feels quite divine.
The moon gives a chuckle, a silvery tease,
I tumble through dreams, swaying in the breeze.

Galaxies giggle as I roam the expanse,
Every twirl and stumble becomes a grand dance.
In the vortex of humor, I find my delight,
Each chance that I take feels perfectly right.

When the universe chuckles, I can't help but grin,
For within all the chaos, joy just begins.
So I'll waltz with the comets and sing with the sun,
In this cosmic ballet, we dance as one.

Dancing with Doubt

In the garden of whims, we sway and spin,
With questions like balloons, floating on a whim.
Each twist and turn, a chuckle we find,
As we trip on the roots, a merry unwind.

The shadows tease us with tales so grand,
Yet lead us in circles, a zany band.
We chase after certainty, slips of our feet,
In this dance of delight, each stumble's a treat.

The Lighthearted Labyrinth

In a maze made of laughter, we skip and we twirl,
Chasing breadcrumbs of joy as the moments unfurl.
With every wrong turn, we erupt into glee,
For the daft little paths are the best place to be.

Each corner we round holds a surprise,
A jester who juggles with comical sighs.
We take off our shoes, let the silliness reign,
In this tangle of thought, there's no room for pain.

Serendipity's Embrace

With serendipity's wink, we wander astray,
Falling in love with the nonsense that plays.
A misstep, a giggle, a pie in the face,
Life's funny little traps, what a charming embrace!

The pebbles we tread on, a slippery crew,
Keep sending us spinning to fortunes anew.
In the folly of chance, we skip hand in hand,
Creating our joy in this whimsical land.

Follies of the Soul

In the follies of being, we boldly parade,
Wearing mismatched socks, an absurd masquerade.
Each blunder we make, a tickle to share,
The soul's giddy laughter floats high in the air.

We juggle our dreams with a splash of disdain,
While moonlight whispers sweet nothings in vain.
Through the carnival of chaos, we sway to and fro,
In the heart of the jest, our spirit will glow.

Bursting Bubbles of Thought

In the realm where giggles play,
Bubbles float, then drift away.
Thoughts like popcorn, popping bright,
Chasing shadows in the light.

Witty whispers tickle, tease,
Making sense of life's unease.
A jester's mind, a playful jest,
Finding joy within the quest.

Philosophers wearing clownish wigs,
Asking questions, dancing jigs.
With each ponder, laughter grows,
Ticklish truths that nobody knows.

In this circus of the mind,
We embrace what we can't find.
With each bubble, thoughts collide,
In giggles, we take it all in stride.

Amusement in Anchors Aweigh

Sail away on ships of dreams,
Where humor flows like bubbling streams.
Anchors aweigh, and spirits soar,
Finding laughter on distant shores.

Navigating with silly maps,
Avoiding serious mishaps.
The crew is jesters, full of cheer,
Sailing through absurd frontier.

Each wave a chuckle, each gust a grin,
With every splash, the fun begins.
We navigate with jesting flair,
Steering boats through the salty air.

In the stars, we spot our fate,
A winking cosmos, never late.
With laughter, we explore and play,
Under skies that gleefully sway.

Ticklish Tidbits of Truth

Hidden nuggets buried deep,
In laughter's arms, we take a leap.
Each little tidbit, a joyful tease,
Unraveling mysteries with ease.

Truth tickles like a feathered quill,
Writing stories that spark the thrill.
With chuckles echoing in the mind,
Serious thoughts left behind.

As we nibble on wisdom's snacks,
Sipping joy from life's bright cracks.
A revelry of thoughts, so sweet,
Matching giggles with every beat.

With curious voices leading the way,
We dig for gems where shadows play.
Finding truth in a jester's rhyme,
Ticklish joy, transcending time.

Mirth on the Marrow

In caverns deep, where humor thrives,
Mirth resides and laughter jives.
Giggling echoes bounce around,
In marrow's depths, delight is found.

Each bone a tale, a quirky jest,
Ticklish stories that never rest.
Tickled ribs and rolling eyes,
In funny bones, the truth lies.

With every crack, a chuckle breaks,
Silly whispers the marrow makes.
In laughter's grip, we boldly dance,
Waltzing with fate in a merry trance.

Through every twist of fate and fun,
We search for meaning, everyone.
Where joys collide, life boldly shows,
In mirth, the marrow of joy grows.

Snickers at the Crossroads of Meaning

In search of wisdom, I took a trip,
With socks that didn't match and a banana slip.
The sage I met wore a jester's hat,
Said, "Life's a stage, just a silly chat!"

Between the signs that point to fate,
I found a taco stand, oh how great!
With every bite of spicy delight,
I pondered deep, then laughed all night.

Emotions swirling like a dizzy kite,
I tripped on thoughts that felt so right.
The meaning's there, or just some cheese?
A giggle fit, with more to seize!

So here I stand at a fork in the road,
With a rubber chicken, my heavy load.
In search of answers, I laugh and roam,
For in this quest, I feel at home.

Jests and Journeys: A Life Unscripted

A compass points, but where's the trail?
With icing on muffins, I start to sail.
The map is wobbly, drawn by a clown,
Who chuckles softly, "Don't let me down!"

Each twist and turn brings giggles abound,
Hitchhiking with a cat, oh what a sound!
It chatters secrets, both sly and sly,
While I contemplate the reason why.

Under moonbeams like bouncing balls,
I slip on meaning and trip on calls.
With laughter echoing in the night,
I dance with shadows, feeling just right.

So come along, just take my hand,
Through the jesting chaos of this land.
A life unscripted, a joyous scheme,
We'll ponder purpose, or so it seems.

The Humorist's Atlas of Existence

With every laugh card in my deck,
I navigate this life, what the heck!
Wandering paths where the wise folks meet,
Trading jokes for truths, quite the feat.

I chart the waters of giggles and grins,
Finding treasure in the follies of sins.
Each map leads to quirky little clues,
A silhouette dance with the existential blues.

The compass spins, yet I'm not afraid,
For beneath the starlight, my plans are laid.
With time as the punchline, I burst into glee,
Every joke tells a story, just wait and see.

So raise your glass, a toast to the quest,
With laughter as fuel, for it's truly the best.
Finding meaning in each silly jest,
In this atlas of life, we're truly blessed.

Tickles in the Tides of Time

Riding the waves of a giggly sea,
Each splash a chuckle, just let it be.
Time dances away, in flip-flops and shorts,
As moments pass like whimsical sports.

The horizon winks with a playful sigh,
Clouds wear smiles, drifting on high.
With every tickle of the salty wind,
I ponder purpose, where shall it begin?

Seagulls squawk with comedic flair,
As I build castles in sandy air.
With buckets of laughter, I scoop the day,
While questions float like driftwood at play.

So let's surf the tides of this wild design,
For in the quest, we spark and shine.
With each giggle, a mystery sown,
In the sands of time, we're never alone.

The Lightness of Discoveries

In dusty books where secrets lie,
A tickling thought flutters by.
With every page, a giggle starts,
The world spins on, with laughing hearts.

A treasure hunt for silly dreams,
Chasing shadows, bursting seams.
A map drawn in crayon and cheer,
Leading us to treasures near.

We stumble upon a wobbly chair,
Whispering secrets suspended in air.
Finding wisdom in a jelly bean,
What strange truths our eyes have seen!

Under the sun, with laughter bold,
The quest is sweet, the path is gold.
Each step a joke, each smile a clue,
In the lightness, we find what's true.

Silly Scribbles of Understanding

With crayons poised, we scribble wide,
Across the page, our thoughts collide.
A doodle here, a giggle there,
Understanding found in playful air.

Painted smiles and jumbled words,
Like flapping wings of clumsy birds.
The meaning hops, it skips, it sways,
In silly scribbles, wisdom plays.

A chalky sun that beams so bright,
Bringing joy to every sight.
With each mishap, a hearty cheer,
We scribble on, our paths are clear.

The art of jest, the code of fun,
In every laugh, our hearts are won.
Each doodle shakes the heavy past,
In silliness, we find our cast.

Jolly Odyssey

Two socks mismatched, our shoes untied,
We set out on our journey wide.
With giggles echoing through the air,
Each episode of joy we share.

A path of pies, a road of jokes,
With wobbly signs and capering folks.
We dance beneath the silly moon,
With laughter strummed like a funny tune.

Filled with snacks and strange surprises,
The world's a stage for bold disguises.
Each stop's a chance for chuckles to bloom,
As we waddle forth, we make joy loom.

So raise a cup of lemonade,
For every blunder, rewards are made.
In our jolly quest, we spin and whirl,
Finding meaning in a laughing swirl.

The Jest of Being

In a world of gadgets and shiny things,
We search for joy that laughter brings.
Through tangled thoughts and silly dreams,
The jest of life is what it seems.

With jelly shoes and hats askew,
Surprises pop and laughter's due.
Each moment is a prank, it's true,
In cheeky grins, we see it through.

We juggle jumbled words, misread signs,
Dance with doubts like playful vines.
Finding gold in breezy glee,
The jest of being sets us free.

So smile wide, and twirl about,
For in the jest, we sing and shout.
Each giggle mapped, each grin a guide,
In life's great jest, we joyfully abide.

Chuckles in the Cosmos

In the starlit sky, I find my place,
A comical dance in this vast space.
Planets wobble with a silly grin,
While comets spin with a joyful spin.

Galaxies swirl in a dizzying twirl,
Asteroids giggle, and stardust swirls.
A cosmic joke wrapped in a smile,
Forever tickling the void all the while.

The Bright Side of Inquiry

Questions bubble like a fizzy drink,
Curiosity darts faster than you think.
What if penguins wore tuxedos at night?
Would the moon giggle at such a sight?

The quest for answers becomes a prank,
With riddles hiding at the bottom of the tank.
A twist of fate brings a cheeky surprise,
In a world where nonsense wears a disguise.

Mirthful Musings

Thoughts dance lightly on a feathered breeze,
Silly ideas swirl with the buzzing bees.
What if dogs held council, sipping tea?
Spouting wisdom while chasing a bee?

Laughter echoes in a garden of dreams,
Where nothing is truly what it seems.
Tickles of truth in every fable spun,
Mirthful musings under the sun.

Finding Bliss in the Abyss

In shadows deep, I flash a grin,
For even darkness has a way to win.
With every tumble into the void,
There lies a chuckle, hard to avoid.

Beneath the depths where the weird fish play,
I stumble upon joy in a curious way.
A wink from the universe, oh so sly,
Finding bliss while I float and fly.

Jokes Among the Journey

A traveler once lost his way,
He asked a tree for advice today.
The tree just chuckled, roots all a-twist,
"You're talking to wood; I'm hard to assist!"

A chicken crossed roads with flair,
To find some wisdom, or is it rare?
It stumbled on a sign with a grin,
"The grass is greener, but you can't eat din!"

An owl surveyed its nightly flight,
It hooted, "Where's the human delight?"
But all it found was a sleeping hare,
With dreams of cheese and a cozy chair.

So on they go, with feet quite spry,
Making jokes under the vast blue sky.
In search of meaning, they spin and twirl,
Each pun a gem in their whimsical whirl.

Frolics of the Heart

A jester danced with grace and flair,
He offered his heart—light as air.
With jokes so silly, laughter's embrace,
He won the crowd in this playful space.

A clown tried to tell the meaning of life,
He tripped on a banana, causing some strife.
With pie in his face, he blurted out loud,
"It's not about sadness; just join the crowd!"

A butterfly laughed at a toad on a log,
"You're smooth as a rock, like a moonlit fog!"
The toad just croaked, "Oh why so bright?"
And twirled in the shadows, avoiding the light.

Through silly smiles, they prance and play,
Each frolic a joy, lighting the way.
In jest they find what hearts truly seek,
A tickle of truth, in laughter they speak.

Truths Wrapped in Whimsy

A wise old fox, with a twinkle in eyes,
Said truths are like pies, one layer in disguise.
Beneath the crust lies a savory core,
These secrets are tasty but leave you wanting more.

A penguin in tuxedo, slick as can be,
Claimed he knew the key to laughter's decree.
With every slip on a slick patch of ice,
He showed the whole world that chaos is nice.

A snail in a race, quite slow on the line,
Said, "Haste makes for trouble—just take your time!"
He laughed as he joined the swift and the spry,
"Life's not a dash, it's a gentle sigh."

So throw back your head and savor the cheer,
In moments of whimsy, the truth is quite clear.
Wrapped in a giggle, with warmth in your heart,
Find meaning in laughter; that's just the start.

Whirls of Witty Wonder

A magician pulled a cat from a hat,
Said, "It's not real magic, just look at that!"
The cat gave a yawn, with a flick of its tail,
And disappeared with a meow, leaving only a trail.

A squirrel shared jokes with friends on a limb,
"Why don't they play cards in the woods? On a whim!"
They crackled with laughter, a busted-up nut,
As leaves clapped above, saying, "What's the rut?"

A goldfish chatted with dreams in a bowl,
"Who says I'm shallow? Just hear my soul!"
It splashed and it swirled, a jest here and there,
All those swimming thoughts, floating in air.

In whirls of delight, they danced and spun,
Each twist a reminder; life's meant for fun.
With wonders untold in their frolicsome quest,
In laughter they find what they cherish the best.

Chortles over the Chasms of Thought

In a world where thoughts collide,
Clowns juggle ideas side by side.
They trip on wisdom, take a fall,
Yet find the humor in it all.

Amidst the chaos, laughter reigns,
As wisdom slips like careless stains.
Philosophers wear rubber shoes,
To dance in puddles of the blues.

Beneath the serious sun so bright,
Silliness shines in the moonlight.
Questions hang like strings of cheese,
While answers tease and aim to please.

With giggles echoing from deep thought,
The merry prankster finds what's sought.
For truth and jest, a grand ballet,
In every chase, it's jest we play.

The Comic Relief of Existence

Each tick of time, a joke unfolds,
A universe of giggles bold.
Cosmic clowns, in their grand show,
Juggle stars just to make us glow.

The meaning's hidden in punchlines bright,
With every folly, we take flight.
Existence dances, light on its toes,
With chuckles sprouting like springtime rose.

A riddle wrapped in comic dare,
We wear our questions, none to spare.
Life's a circus, don't you see?
A laughter ring of mystery.

So here we stand, with grins so wide,
In this nutty universe, we'll bide.
For every riddle and twist we find,
A chuckle echoes, sweet and kind.

Giggles in the Garden of Inquiry

In the garden where thoughts grow free,
We plant our questions like a tree.
The blooms of laughter, bright and bold,
Unravel secrets yet untold.

With giddy bees that buzz about,
They collect chuckles, roundabout.
As petals fall like whispered dreams,
We find the joy in all that seems.

Each leaf a riddle, green and lush,
In the breeze, ideas rush.
We water doubts, let laughter sprout,
In this whimsical space, devoid of doubt.

So wander through this playful plot,
Where questions mingle, never caught.
With every jest that fills the air,
We bloom in joy, without a care.

Reveling in the Riddles of Reality

Reality's a puzzle piece,
With laughter as the sweet release.
Jesters jump through hoops of thought,
In every twist, new jokes are caught.

Amidst the serious, we will sway,
Unravel truths in the silliest way.
Each conundrum, like a dancing flame,
Lights up the path, ignites the game.

With riddles wrapped in giggles bright,
We chase the shadows in the light.
Chaos sings a curious tune,
As jesters waltz beneath the moon.

So here's to joy, in all its forms,
In every riddle, laughter storms.
For life's a stage, and we the show,
With humor as our hearts' warm glow.

The Joyful Inquiry

Upon a hill, the seekers play,
They chase the dawn, they greet the day.
With riddles tossed like frisbees bright,
They ponder life in pure delight.

A cat in sunglasses struts with pride,
While squirrels debate, they won't abide.
Their giggles echo through the trees,
As questions swirl like playful bees.

The moon peeks in with a curious grin,
As wise old owls join in the din.
With wisecracks sharp, and jests that shine,
They sip on tea, discussing the divine.

In every laugh, a bit of truth,
As dreams collide with the funny youth.
They dance around in a merry spree,
The answers hide where laughter be.

Murmurs of Mirth

In a coffee shop, ideas brew,
A poet spills some thoughts askew.
With laughter bubbling in his cup,
He scribbles down, then lifts it up.

A dog in a bowtie steals the show,
His antics spark a joyful flow.
With every wag, he seems to say,
Life's best enjoyed in a silly way.

In jumbled words and tangled lines,
The search for truth is where fun shines.
Like clowns who juggle fickle dreams,
They find the sense amidst the beams.

In every giggle lies a clue,
A playful nudge to see it through.
With mirth and cheer, they sing and sway,
Finding meaning in the light of day.

Revelations Wrapped in Riddles

Behind a bush, a fox does muse,
He whispers secrets we can't refuse.
With riddles wrapped in a funny tale,
He spins his yarn without a fail.

A penguin winks with a comical nod,
As he flops around like an awkward God.
His antics keep the world at bay,
Searching for meaning in a jolly way.

The stars above giggle in delight,
As shadows dance upon the night.
Each twinkling spark a merry tease,
Inviting seekers to question with ease.

In every riddle, a spark of glee,
As laughter leads to mystery.
Through nonsense and jest, the seekers find,
The joy of truth in the playful mind.

The Happy Hodgepodge

A jumble sale of dreams and schemes,
Where nothing's ever as it seems.
With mismatched socks and hats askew,
They search for meaning, just for you.

A giraffe with glasses reads the news,
While chickens dance in silly shoes.
Their laughter rings like bells that chime,
As they untangle the threads of time.

With crayons bright and paints that splash,
They fill the world with a joyful dash.
Every canvas tells a tale anew,
Of seeking paths that break in two.

In this hodgepodge of whims and wits,
The cosmos chuckles, as it fits.
For in the chaos, there's much to glean,
The joy of life, both wild and keen.

The Funhouse of Reflection

In mirrors that warp, I twist and I turn,
With every odd shape, a lesson to learn.
Giggles emerge from the quirks of the glass,
Where wisdom is silly, and shadows amass.

The reflections I see make me ponder and grin,
As each wiggly visage reveals what's within.
I trip on my thoughts, and I giggle aloud,
In this wacky funhouse, I stand out, so proud.

Every image a joke, every laugh a delight,
Between silly blunders, I find weird insight.
The laughter resounds, a riddle in jest,
In the maze of my mind, I'm eternally blessed.

So, step in my world where the nonsense is grand,
We'll dance through the chaos, hand in hand.
The funhouse of thought echoes glee through the night,
In this carnival of meaning, everything feels right.

Jests of the Journey

With a map that's all scribbles and directions unclear,
I ponder on pathways while sipping my beer.
Each twist in the road brings a chuckle or two,
As life's silly puzzles keep changing the view.

I trip on a stone that once claimed to be wise,
And fall in a bush to my own sweet surprise.
The creatures I meet wave with funny faces,
In this carnival of life, there are plenty of places.

My feet seem to dance with a mind of their own,
As laughter erupts in this realm I've been shown.
The jests of the journey are treasures so rare,
In the simplest moments, I feel light as air.

So let's wander together, with giggles in tow,
With joy woven deeply in each step we go.
The path is a tease, with a wink and a pun,
In the laughter of living, we've already won.

Echoes of Exuberance

Amidst the tall trees, with laughter I roam,
In each rustling leaf lies a secretive tome.
The echoes that giggle weave wisdom so bright,
In the canopy's hush, my heart takes to flight.

Beneath every branch, a pun waits to leap,
With whispers of joy that make shadows creep.
A chorus of chuckles wraps 'round like a quilt,
In the forest of thoughts, my fears start to wilt.

I chase after rainbows with socks made of cheer,
Splashing in puddles, detecting no fear.
Every droplet of humor shines brightly and clear,
In this echoing woodland, I hold laughter dear.

The exuberance calls as I skip through the glades,
With giggles my guide in these magical shades.
Each moment is timeless, and each laugh is a gift,
In the echoes of joy, my spirit takes lift.

The Merry Mix of Mystery

In a pot full of quirks, I stir up the fun,
With secrets that bubble under the sun.
A pinch of absurd, a dash of delight,
In this merry mix, the odd feels just right.

The riddles I toss are like sugar on cakes,
With every sweet bite, a wonder awakes.
I've found that the strange can be deeply profound,
In the layers of laughter, new meanings abound.

The whirls and the twirls of this whimsical blend,
Invite every heart to jump in and transcend.
From questions of purpose to jests we can share,
The mystery swirls in a playful affair.

So let's dance with the bizarre and skip down the lane,
With humor our compass, there's no room for pain.
In the merry mix cooking up laughter and glee,
We'll uncover the magic of just being free.

Laughter Beneath Starry Skies

Under a moon that winks at me,
I dance like a leaf on a playful spree.
Stars chuckle bright in the twilight glow,
Tickling the night as the breezes blow.

Midnight confessions to the shimmering dust,
Where dreams and giggles twirl and gust.
The cosmos laughs, sparking joy so high,
In this celestial jest, time flutters by.

Each twinkle a joke, each shadow a jest,
With cosmic punchlines, we laugh with zest.
We whisper our secrets to the twinkling vast,
And find in the night, a bond unsurpassed.

So, let's toast to laughter beneath the dome,
In this merry pursuit, we'll always find home.
Under the sky, our hearts lift and sway,
As joy wraps around us, come what may.

The Joyful Jester in Search of Truth

A jester prances with a grin so wide,
His pockets full of laughter, he takes in stride.
With floppy shoes and a heart so light,
He twirls through shadows, igniting the night.

With every riddle, a giggle breaks free,
Chasing the wisdom that only fools see.
He juggles soft dreams and hopes on a string,
In the pursuit of truth, he finds joy to bring.

He spins tales of folly with whimsical flair,
Dancing with nonsense that hangs in the air.
In mirrors of laughter, reflections reveal,
The heart of the quest is the joy that we feel.

So, trust in the jester with tricks to unfold,
For in every jest, a true truth can be told.
Through giggles and grins, he reminds with a cheer,
Life's a grand jest, so let's laugh while we're here.

Whispers of Glee in the Wilderness

In the woods where the critters play tag,
The bushes hum tunes, letting joy brag.
Squirrels drop acorns, a laughter-filled show,
As shadows waltz lightly, the stars start to glow.

Beneath leafy arches, we skip with delight,
Telling tall tales to the hush of the night.
Each rustle and giggle, a secret to share,
In nature's embrace, we shed every care.

The wind laughs softly, tickling the trees,
As we chase the sunflowers swaying with ease.
With every step forward, we gather a smile,
In whispers of glee, we pause for a while.

So come wander with me, let joy be our guide,
Through wilderness wonders, let laughter reside.
In the heart of the forest, we'll find what is true,
With whispers of glee, just me and you.

Chasing Giggles in the Maze of Existence

In a maze made of laughs, we bound and weave,
With every turn taken, more joy we conceive.
Walls echo chuckles, a pathway adorned,
With jesters and whispers our hearts are warmed.

We tumble through twists with glee as our map,
Turning corners of hope, avoiding the sap.
Each dead end a joke, each loop a delight,
In this labyrinth of life, everything feels right.

The signs read 'giggle' and 'smile' ahead,
As we dance through the paths that curiosity led.
With every new corner, a burst of surprise,
In the maze of existence, joy never dies.

So let's skip down this road paved with cheer,
In pursuit of the laughter that always draws near.
Together we'll wander, with no need for maps,
In this whimsical quest, we'll close with some laughs.

The Silliest Steps on a Serious Path

With floppy shoes and hats so tall,
We dance upon life's silly ball.
The road is bent, the path is wide,
We'll trip and cheer, let's take the ride.

Each serious thought takes flight on wings,
A jest can heal what sorrow brings.
With every stumble, laughter's near,
We'll turn our woes to gleeful cheer.

In search of truth, we play a game,
Where every joke ignites a flame.
Through twists and turns, we skip and sway,
The silliest steps will light our way.

So clap your hands and stomp your feet,
Embrace the fun, the heart's quick beat.
For life's a jest, a merry show,
With joy, we flourish and ever grow.

Humor as a Lantern in the Fog

In clouds of doubt, a beacon gleams,
With laughter's glow, we weave our dreams.
Fog swirls around like cotton candy,
Yet humor lights the night uncanny.

A slip upon the stones we'll make,
But giggles rise, no hearts will break.
With every chuckle, shadows flee,
A lantern's warmth, just wait and see.

Jokes like fireflies in the dusk,
Reveal the gems we often husk.
Through foggy paths, we'll dance and twirl,
And paint our lives in shades of pearl.

So grab the torch and lead the way,
With laughter's spark, we'll seize the day.
For humor shines, both bright and strong,
A guiding light where we belong.

Jokes and Journeys of the Soul

We wander far with hearts so light,
In search of laughs that spark delight.
From mountain tops to valleys low,
With every joke, we steal the show.

The soul's a compass, spinning round,
In every chuckle, truth is found.
We trade our worries for a jest,
And find our way, it's for the best.

In playful banter, wisdom hides,
As laughter flows like ocean tides.
With goofy hats and silly rhymes,
Our souls unite across the climes.

So take a step, embrace the jest,
In every giggle, we feel blessed.
For joy will guide our weary path,
With jokes in hand, we'll share the laugh.

The Clown's Footprints on the Sands of Time

With painted smiles and floppy shoes,
The clown's bright path gives us the clues.
In grains of sand, his footprints shine,
Each step a giggle, every line.

Through fleeting moments, he will prance,
Transforming woes into a dance.
His joy spills forth like waves that crash,
A splash of fun, a hearty laugh.

Time moves swift, yet he remains,
A jester's charm as life explains.
Each footprint marks a tale we've missed,
In every giggle, the world's sweet twist.

So gather 'round and hear the sound,
Of laughter woven all around.
For in the sands of life, you'll find,
The clown's warm heart, forever kind.

Snickers of the Soul

In a world of questions, we tumble and twist,
Puns fly like arrows, you get hit and you missed.
Chasing our thoughts like a butterfly's dance,
Who knew the answers went on a prance?

We ponder and giggle, our minds in a flurry,
Each thought a joke, never dare to hurry.
In wisdom's pursuit, we trip on our feet,
Finding the comical in troubles so sweet.

As we quest for the truth, oh what a delight,
The riddles we solve bring laughter so bright.
With every wrong turn, there's humor to find,
A joke in the mess, it's all intertwined.

So chase those snickers, let your spirit breathe,
For meaning is best when it's taken with ease.
At the heart of our search lies a joke so rare,
In the laughter we share, we discover we care.

Enigma with a Smile

With curious faces, we seek out the jest,
Enigmas that tickle, each thought a fun quest.
Around every corner, a riddle does bloop,
Laughter erupts like a cheerful old troupe.

A question, a giggle, the universe winks,
Are we all just bubbles? Oh, what do you think?
In this vast comic circus, we waddle and sway,
Collecting the chuckles that brighten our day.

The meaning, it eludes like a cat in a tree,
While we roll on the ground, just you wait and see!
Each riddle unraveled, a poke in the side,
For deeper truths hide where the humor resides.

What's up with the cosmos? It has quite the laugh,
Life's puzzle is sprinkled with warmth, and some gaff.
Smile wide at the questions, enjoy the surprise,
For joy is the answer that twinkles in eyes.

Quips Under the Stars

Beneath the night sky, we gather in mirth,
Each star a wisecrack, each laugh a rebirth.
We ponder the cosmos, look up with a grin,
Wishing upon comets that dance and spin.

In search of a meaning that twinkles with light,
We trip on our thoughts like a silly kite flight.
The enormous blank canvas invites a good quip,
For the cosmos is vast, let's take a fun trip!

With each little wonder, our giggles erupt,
As questions keep dancing, we happily sup.
Instead of stress, we'll sip on a glee,
Finding our answers in cosmic esprit.

So here's to the quips passed 'round under stars,
In pondering joy, we uncover who we are.
Let laughter be lanterns that guide us along,
As we traverse the night with our whimsical song.

The Funny Side of Philosophy

When pondering existence, we grin and we sway,
For wisdom can tickle in such a fun way.
Questions like bubbles, they float in the air,
Making us giggle as we ponder and dare.

A philosopher's pencil, it scribbles and dives,
Into thoughts that can twist, yet somehow it thrives.
The absurdity flares with each paradox found,
In the amusing confusions, new truths can abound.

Why worry with logic when humor is clear?
In the quest for the meaning, let's share a good cheer.
Embrace every chuckle, let laughter entice,
In the punchline of life, find your very own spice.

So dance with the queries and giggle aloud,
The serious moments can wear quite a shroud.
Underneath all the pondering, bright smiles will show,
That the funny side's waiting, so let it all flow.

Grinning in the Dark

In shadows where the giggles play,
A silly thought will lead the way.
The moon joins in with a wink so bright,
While owls chuckle through the night.

We chase our dreams with silly prance,
A dance of joy, a jolly chance.
Each stumble's met with joyous glee,
As we spin around, just you and me.

We search for signs in the starlit sky,
And wonder why the cat's so spry.
With every twist, we laugh aloud,
Our doubts dissolve beneath a cloud.

So in the dark, let's hoot and cheer,
For in our hearts, the light is near.
Emboldened by our playful spree,
We find our truth with glee and glee.

Chortles of the Conscious

A tickle found in wisdom's chest,
The mind will jest, it loves the jest.
With quirky thoughts that spring awake,
We ride the waves of giggling fate.

In serious halls where thinkers dwell,
A chuckle echoes, casting a spell.
Philosophers grin like children so spry,
Their theories dance like butterflies.

A question asked with a wink so wide,
Brings forth answers we cannot hide.
As laughter bends the heavy air,
We glimpse the truth beyond despair.

For wisdom springing from quaint delight,
Turns heavy burdens to feathers light.
So let us chortle, let us jest,
In this grand game, it's all a fest!

The Giddy Pursuit

In pursuit of what we cannot see,
We skip along with wild glee.
With every turn, a comic prize,
A treasure hunt beneath bright skies.

With maps all drawn in crayon hues,
We stumble forth in misfit shoes.
The compass spins, the laughter flies,
As we chase the whims of silly skies.

A joke, a riddle, a playful pun,
We chase the dusk, we chase the sun.
Each giggle leads to winding trails,
Where nonsense blooms and laughter sails.

The quest may twist, but we don't fret,
With every pitfall, there's no regret.
In the giddy chase, our hearts unite,
And through it all, we find delight.

Hilarity in Harmony

When all seems grim, and skies are gray,
We sing out loud, come what may.
With harmonies of silly cheer,
We craft our joys, we have no fear.

The notes may waver, but hearts will soar,
Through every line, we crave much more.
In laughter's wake, we journey far,
With friendship close, our guiding star.

In sync we dance, a merry throng,
As giggles weave the sweetest song.
A symphony of smiles bestowed,
Together we'll lift this flavored load.

So here we stand, in jests we bind,
Embracing life, the love we find.
With every chord, let joy ignite,
In harmony, we take our flight.

The Snickered Quest

In a land where questions dance,
We trip on thoughts that prance.
With every stumble, joy ignites,
In quirky shadows, laughter bites.

Maps of giggles guide the way,
As we search for truth today.
The signs all read, 'Don't take it so,
Just swirl and twirl, let the chuckles flow.'

Silly riddles float on air,
Caught in moments we don't share.
With each mishap, wisdom sneaks,
In chuckles soft, it gently speaks.

Around the bends of blunders wide,
We find the humor's endless tide.
With every jest, we find the key,
Unlocking treasures, wild and free.

The Happy Hurdle

Over hills of wobbly quirks,
We bounce through life with playful smirks.
Each leap a chance to giggle loud,
In silly chaos, we stand proud.

Through puddles deep and fields of glee,
We run the race, just you and me.
With every hurdle, joy's our guide,
In fits of laughter, we confide.

The finish line, a jolly treat,
Where silly songs and friends all meet.
We'll celebrate the stumbles shared,
For in the fun, no heart is scared.

So come along, let's skip and sway,
With happy hearts, we'll find our way.
In every oops, a lesson lives,
Wrapped in smiles, the universe gives.

Winks of Wisdom

A wink from time, as moments play,
Whispers secrets in the fray.
Don't take it serious, just unwind,
The paths of laughter are hard to find.

Marble wisdoms, cracked and bright,
Show us joy in the weirdest light.
With every eyebrow raised, we see,
The funny truth inside the glee.

Jokes and jests, like stars they shine,
Lighting the way, oh so fine.
In every giggle, stories dwell,
Of how we laugh, and all is well.

So twirl with fate, embrace the jest,
In the riddle of life, we're truly blessed.
With every moment shared and sweet,
The winks of wisdom make us complete.

The Chuckle of Curiosity

In the garden of quirky thoughts,
Curiosity blooms, tying knots.
With every question, we draw near,
A chuckle echoes, loud and clear.

What's that laughter beneath the moon?
A riddle sung, a playful tune.
With each discovery, giggles grow,
Revealing secrets we didn't know.

A treasure chest of silly clues,
Hidden paths that lead to whos.
Through twists and turns, we trek with cheer,
In absurdity, the truth draws near.

So let's embrace the chuckle's charm,
As we search for meaning, side by side, warm.
In every giggle, wonder thrives,
Curiosity, where joy arrives.

Chasing Joyful Shadows

In search of smiles that come and go,
I trip on dreams, to steal the show.
With clumsy feet and splendid cheer,
I dance with shadows, never fear.

The world's a joke, a silly game,
Where questions linger, yet no one's lame.
We tumble through absurdity's weave,
Chasing giggles that never leave.

A rubber chicken's on the run,
A punchline hidden in the sun.
I chase horizons that wink and tease,
In this mad race, I find my ease.

With every step, I'm bound to grin,
What's life without a cheeky spin?
With joyful shadows all around,
In laughter's arms, I'm glory-bound.

Playful Ponderings

Bubbles bounce in a springtime breeze,
Thoughts take flight, just like the bees.
In silly hats, we ponder fate,
With every giggle, it feels so great.

What's the meaning of all we see?
A riddle wrapped in glee, you see.
We toss our socks in cosmic air,
And wonder if the stars would care.

Frogs in bowties croak the tunes,
While dancing turtles tease the moons.
With hearts so light, we strut and prance,
The universe joins in the dance.

Questions swirl like candy floss,
In this grand race, there's never loss.
Playful ponderings fill the space,
As laughter leads us through the chase.

The Comedy of Existence

Life's a stage with wobbly sets,
Where punchlines bloom, and no one frets.
In every twist, a giggle hides,
While fortune never takes sides.

A jester's cap upon my head,
I juggle thoughts, both light and dread.
What's serious is simply absurd,
In this mad play, nothing's blurred.

To trip on truths that make us grin,
We fall, get up, and dive right in.
In cosmic jest, we find our part,
With jigsaw pieces for the heart.

So here's a toast to life's great jest,
With cackles loud, we're truly blessed.
Together in this merry scene,
We weave the threads of what's unseen.

Giggles Among the Stars

Stars twinkle in their velvet dance,
Inviting us to take a chance.
With cosmic giggles, we float and sway,
In the vastness, we find our way.

Asteroids with silly grins zoom by,
As comets tail and joyful sigh.
In the galaxy's whims, we dive,
Here in this jest, we come alive.

Planets spin with a cheeky flair,
While we share secrets in the air.
Under the moon's grin, we take flight,
With stardust dreams that feel just right.

In laughter's orbit, we find our place,
We frolic through the cosmic race.
Among the stars, we giggle bright,
In this celestial giggle, we find our light.

Witty Whispers of Wisdom

In a world of queries wide,
We search for truth with humor spied.
A chuckle here, a giggle there,
Wisdom wrapped in laughter's flair.

Each riddle cracked with a pun so bright,
Questions softened by joy's delight.
Through curious paths, we wander and roam,
Finding wit in the unknown dome.

So let us dance with each silly phase,
Amid the chaos, we'll find our ways.
In every jest, a lesson dwells,
In laughter's arms, our spirit swells.

With gentle nudges from funny lines,
Life's complexity with humor shines.
For wisdom's often in playful guise,
With laughter echoing 'neath wise skies.

Laughs that Illuminate

In shadows deep, we seek the light,
With chuckling hearts, we take flight.
Each silly step, a sign we trace,
Joy is etched on every face.

The answers hide in laughter's glow,
A giggle shared as we all grow.
In every quirk and playful jest,
We find ourselves, we feel the best.

So here's to laughs that lift us high,
To moments bright that make us sigh.
Exploring thought with a grin so wide,
In silly adventures, we confide.

Wonder wrapped in a punchline's cheer,
Truths revealed when humor's near.
In the tapestry of life's great game,
We paint for joy, not just for fame.

Silliness of Searching

In the maze of thoughts, we scurry about,
With a chuckle here, a little pout.
We blunder, we babble, oh what a sight,
Finding clarity in the quirky night.

Flip-flopped questions, confusing and fun,
Each misstep leads to a brighter sun.
With jests like breadcrumbs, we trail behind,
Discovering treasures in the playful mind.

What's the meaning? We laugh, we jest,
With each silly query, we're truly blessed.
In moments of whimsy, our spirits play,
Silliness shows us a brighter way.

So let us wander with grins on our face,
In the quest for joy, we find our place.
Each giggle a guiding star's soft embrace,
In the silliness, life finds its grace.

The Jaunt of Joy

On roads of laughter, we skip and sway,
With every step, we find a way.
In jumbles of words, we twist and twirl,
Life's grand jest, like a merry whirl.

Searching high and diving low,
For meaning missed in the ebb and flow.
With humor sprouting in every crack,
There's wisdom brewing, no need to lack.

Our bags packed full of giggles and cheer,
In moments shared, nothing to fear.
Here's to the journey, so wild and free,
In the jaunt of joy, we'll simply be.

So let's raise our voices, let laughter reign,
In this dance of life, there's much to gain.
With each silly stride, we gather the light,
On this quest together, everything's bright.

Joking with the Universe

In a space of cosmic whim,
Stars winking, light years dim.
I asked the moon for wisdom bright,
It replied with a playful bite.

Black holes giggle, planets spin,
Tickled by the chaos within.
Galaxies swirl in a jolly dance,
Finding joy in the vast expanse.

A comet whizzed, a cheeky grin,
"Catch me if you can, begin!"
I waved my hand, it swirled and played,
In the universe, humor displayed.

So I roam in this stellar jest,
Finding jokes that never rest.
In every twinkle, every gleam,
The cosmos laughs, it's quite the dream.

Trials of a Merry Mind

With a hat made of sunbeams bright,
I tackle puzzles with sheer delight.
A riddle whispered on the breeze,
Solving it brings such easy tease.

I stumbled on a bridge of sighs,
Chased by shadows, no surprise.
Yet even in the darkest woe,
I trip and tumble, all aglow.

Wisdom's a clown with painted face,
Cracking jokes on this winding chase.
Laughter dances in my brain,
Turning trials into silly gains.

Each step a play, each fall a jest,
I wear my troubles like a fest.
In every stumble, life's design,
A merry mind, so fine, divine.

Lively Lessons of the Unknown

In the shadows where secrets hide,
A giggle echoes, never denied.
Lessons bubble like soda pop,
Catch the fizz before it drops!

Unfurling truths in a silly guise,
Mysteries dance before our eyes.
With every twist, a chuckle comes,
The unknown thrives where laughter hums.

Adventure calls with a playful wink,
What lies ahead—oh, let me think!
Each wrong turn is a tale to tell,
As we tumble down this joy-filled well.

So here I stand, at the edge of fun,
Eager for lessons yet to run.
With every step into the blight,
The unknown sparkles, oh what a sight!

Smiles Beneath the Surface

Beneath the waves of thought I dive,
Searching for smiles, feeling alive.
Coral reefs of quirky ideas,
Glimmering bright like giggling cheers.

Tangled seaweed plays on the tide,
Poking fun, there's no need to hide.
A dolphin flips with a cheeky wink,
Showing me more than I might think.

Every bubble carries a tune,
Rising upward, a lightened boon.
Beneath the surface, joy runs deep,
In every swirl, the secrets leap.

So I dive down with glee and zest,
Currents of laughter, never rest.
In the ocean's heart, I'll always seek,
Smiles await, and they speak.

Joyful Journeys through the Unknown

With each step forward, a skip in the beat,
The map is a joke, not a guide to retreat.
Clouds dance in laughter, sun beams with flair,
Lost in the moment, with no need to care.

Pockets of wonders, we gather like seeds,
Bumper cars of fate, we fill up our needs.
Every turn's a riddle, we chuckle and move,
In the realm of surprise, we find our groove.

Beneath the starlight, the shadows do play,
We chase after dreams that lead us astray.
Exquisite confusion becomes quite the game,
Each twist of the path, we laugh just the same.

So tiptoe through life with a grin and a wink,
The unknown's a canvas, much brighter than ink.
With joys uncharted, let merriment flow,
In the heart of the voyage, there's more to bestow.

The Fool's Guide to Finding Wisdom

One must be silly, oh what a delight,
To juggle the lessons in the glow of night.
With socks as a crown and a grin ear to ear,
We stumble through wisdom, the path becomes clear.

The wise ones will frown, but we giggle in jest,
For truth dressed in laughter is truly the best.
With mismatched old shoes and a feathered cap,
Finding profound thoughts wrapped in a nap.

Turn every misstep into a dance on the floor,
The more that you twirl, the more you'll explore.
A plunge into nonsense, the philosopher's dream,
An absurd little giggle flows into a stream.

So grab a balloon, it will guide you today,
Through the fields of the foolish, we prance and we play.
In wisdom united, we frolic and sing,
In the folly of life, oh, hear laughter ring!

Grins Along the Unpaved Road

On roads that are bumpy, we hop and we roll,
With giggles of joy, we embrace every hole.
A detour of laughter leads us far and wide,
In each rut or bump, we take it in stride.

With a map made of scribbles and doodles that cheer,
We greet every mishap with a hearty laugh here.
The horizon is winking, the sky gives a poke,
In the arc of the journey, we tease and we joke.

Rolling down hills with the thrill of the breeze,
Our hearts chase the humor like leaves in the trees.
We trip on the funny, we fall, then we rise,
Each page of this tale, a joyous surprise.

So gather your friends, let's wander and roam,
In the chaos of joy, we build our own home.
Every turn tells a story where giggles abound,
In the dance of diversion, pure joy can be found.

Whimsy in the Depths of Reflection

In the mirror of thoughts, odd shapes come to play,
Where ponderings twist in a brightly odd way.
A wink from the shadows, a grin from the light,
In reflections we gather, all quirky and bright.

With musings like bubbles that float in the air,
In flights of imagination, we land with a flare.
Questioning seriousness with every small pause,
Embracing absurdity, just because!

So let's leap into dreams, a jump and a twirl,
With mirth in our hearts, watch the thoughts whirl.
In every deep thought, a punchline that's near,
We laugh through the pathways that lead us to here.

So tease out the worries, let whimsy abound,
In depths of reflection, pure joy can be found.
With giggles as guides, this quest won't be grim,
In the fun of our searching, we'll dance and we'll swim.

Chirps of Cheerful Curiosity

In a world of wobbling wonders,
We bounce on clouds like springs.
Chirping dreams in vibrant colors,
As the curious birdie sings.

Each question hops like a bunny,
With answers hidden like cheese.
Laughter dances, bright and sunny,
In the playful rustle of leaves.

We chase the shadows of silly thoughts,
With a net made of giggles tight.
In the garden where bright wisdom sprouts,
The bees buzz about, full of delight.

So let's twirl on this merry ride,
With feet that tickle the grass.
Where absurdity and joy collide,
And time slips away in a flash.

Tickles of Thought

In the attic of my silly head,
Thoughts are bouncing on a beam.
Like popcorn kernels, they pop instead,
Of straying far from the dream.

A jester's cap, a floppy shoe,
Each idea juggles in a line.
Tickling brains with something new,
As we sip our fizzy brine.

Let's chase the whims of our fancy,
With giggles trailing in the air.
Witty whispers that feel so chancy,
Bring merriment beyond compare.

So grab your hat and wear it proud,
We're off to see the funny sights.
Amidst this gleeful, loving crowd,
We'll giggle through the starry nights.

Jestful Jaunts

On paths of whimsy, we prance and play,
Each step a skip, each turn a twirl.
With pockets of jokes to greet the day,
And a hop in the heart of the world.

The trees wear hats made of laughter,
As clouds bounce like fluffy sheep.
In this land, there's no disaster,
Just smiles and secrets we keep.

As we wander through fields of delight,
Every tickle of grass feels right.
With a wink to the sun, so bold and bright,
Our jestful jaunt is pure, unplanned delight.

Hold tight to joy as we roam the lane,
For in each twist, giggles reign.
From silly slips to playful gains,
Our hearts will dance without refrain.

Amusing Angles of Existence

In a world where the oddities shine,
We wear our quirks like a crown.
With each amusing twist and line,
We turn frowns upside down.

The clocks tick backwards, just for fun,
As the moon laughs at the sun.
Painted smiles make the day so light,
In a waltz of whimsy, we unite.

Curved roads lead to laughter spots,
With signs that say, "Take a chance!"
In the garden of thoughts, we plant our plots,
And dance like it's our last romance.

So take a breath and join the spree,
In this circus of joyful friends.
Where every chuckle is pure and free,
And the magic of meaning never ends.

Finding Sunshine in the Labyrinth

In a maze made of jitter and jest,
I tripped on my thoughts, what a mess!
Puppies and rainbows dance in my mind,
Chasing shadows that I cannot find.

Twists and turns with giggles and sighs,
A map drawn in crayon, oh how it lies!
Each corner I turn, another surprise,
Jokes carve the path, not just alibis.

Laughter echoes, a balm for the soul,
Can this be the end? No, just a stroll.
I chase the sun, it chases me back,
In this wacky world, there's no time to slack.

Joy dances here in a carousel's spin,
Every wrong turn is just where I begin.
Navigating with chuckles, a whimsical flight,
Finding sunshine, oh what a delight!

Dancing with Dilemma and Delight

Between choices strewn like confetti of fate,
I tango with worries, oh isn't it great!
Spinning in circles, I trip over choice,
Listening closely, my confusion's voice.

Should I wear polka dots or stripes today?
In such dilemmas, I just laugh and play.
Round and round, in my own little whirl,
Life's a party where chaos can twirl.

With each uncertain step, I find the groove,
A two-step of joy that helps me improve.
Catch me if you can, in this zany ballet,
With a tickle of fate, I dance all day.

Delight in the struggles, it's all a façade,
Turns out my worries have quite the charade.
In the rainbow of chaos, I find my way,
With laughter as guide, it's the best kind of play!

The Silly Melodies of Solitude

In the quiet corners where giggles reside,
I hum silly songs with no shame or hide.
The cat joins my chorus, tail high in the air,
Together we croon, without a care.

Whistling tunes that don't quite align,
My solo concert, oh isn't it fine?
The furniture sways, must be the beat,
A waltz with my shadow, oh what a feat!

Echoes of laughter bounce off the walls,
As I trip on my thoughts, and back I crawl.
A jester in my own quirky scene,
In this little chaos, I'm a queen.

Melodies of solitude, sweet silly song,
In the dance of the night, I feel I belong.
Wrapping in laughter, I twirl and I spin,
In the silence of joy, I've already won.

Laughter's Cloak on Life's Adventure

Clutching my cloak that's patched with glee,
Every laugh a reason, wild and free.
Through valleys of jest and mountains so tall,
Each giggle a reason to have a ball.

The compass of chuckles points everywhere,
Guided by humor, without a care.
Through thick jungles of worries, I prance,
With life as my partner, I lead the dance.

Quirky encounters dress my tale,
I'm a joker in this heroic scale.
With every wrong turn, a punchline blooms,
In this grand adventure, laughter consumes.

So zip up my cloak, let's wander anew,
In the quest of the curious, there's always a view.
With a hearty laugh echoing our call,
Adventure awaits, we shall conquer it all!

The Comedic Compass of Life's Journey

With every twist, a chuckle flows,
A map of mishaps, laughter grows.
Winding paths of silly fate,
Where gaffes and giggles patiently wait.

Jokes are signs on this wild ride,
Navigating with humor as our guide.
Through valleys of blunders, we skip,
Each punchline a treasure, on this trip.

In crew of jesters, hearts collide,
Tickling truths we can't deride.
With a wink, we leap through dark,
Finding giggles in every lark.

So let's embrace the bumpy lanes,
Where folly dances and joy reigns.
With mirth as our compass, we won't stray,
In this comical journey, come what may.

Grinning Among Shadows of Doubt

In the darkness where worries creep,
A grin emerges, wide and deep.
Shadows whisper tales of fright,
Yet we chuckle, turning wrongs to right.

Each tremor brings a punchline near,
Finding humor in what we fear.
With laughs like lanterns, we illuminate,
Navigating gloom with a jovial gait.

Wobbly paths, they ebb and flow,
But with every slip, we learn to glow.
Unseen fears that loom so tall,
With playful jests, we will not fall.

In the echo of doubts, we find our tune,
And dance among the elements, like a cartoon.
For laughter's the lantern, fierce and bright,
Guiding us safely through the night.

Smiles as Maps in the Unknown

In tangled woods, a grin appears,
Leading us through the maze of fears.
Each smile a marker, bold and clear,
Pointing the way with silliness near.

Mysterious realms where giggles soar,
We collect chuckles like treasures galore.
With each step, a funny tale is spun,
Mapping the path where joy is won.

Echoes of laughter fill the air,
As we wander without a care.
In this land of whimsy, we roam,
Finding adventure wherever we comb.

So let's flaunt our quirks, our shining faces,
Guided by smiles through odd places.
Each laugh a beacon, bright and free,
Navigating life's absurdity.

Playful Echoes Across the Abyss

Over the edge, the abyss does call,
With fears that threaten to make us fall.
Yet echoes of laughter ripple the air,
Bouncing back with humor's flair.

As we peer into the void so vast,
We find joy in shadows that are cast.
With every giggle, we slip and slide,
Dancing on the edge, our laughter our guide.

In the depths where silly whispers play,
We munch on the absurd, in a playful way.
In this game of life, we take our chance,
Swaying to the rhythm of a comic dance.

So let's leap with glee across the brink,
Find joy in the chaos, let our spirits sync.
For in the echoes of our giggling bliss,
We discover meaning in the abyss.

Jovial Journeys

On the road with socks that clash,
A cheerful grin, a silly splash.
Maps upside down, we lose our way,
Yet every turn brings a new display.

Chasing clouds that look like bread,
Imagining them toasted instead.
With every bend, a prank unfolds,
Laughter as rich as treasure gold.

Comical detours mark the path,
A running joke, we've found the math.
We twirl and dance through fields of green,
And leave behind the serious scene.

In the end, it's not the goal,
But every giggle that makes us whole.
So pack your dreams with silly schemes,
And let's chase life, a world of dreams.

Whimsical Wisdom

Beneath the stars we craft our tales,
With quirky minds and joyful wails.
The universe whispers jokes so grand,
We giggle at the vastness, hand in hand.

A wise old owl with mismatched shoes,
Gives sage advice with a laugh in hues.
"Dance in the rain, embrace the splash,
Life's a riddle, don't make it a clash!"

A wobbly chair, a stubborn cat,
Teach us secrets in a jovial chat.
With every stumble, a lesson learned,
In the joy of life, our hearts are turned.

So let's wear frowns like silly hats,
And chase our worries like playful cats.
For in the funny, we find the truth,
Whimsical wisdom, eternal youth.

The Search for Smiles

In gardens wild with flowers bright,
We hunt for giggles, pure delight.
With every step, a tickling breeze,
Collecting grins like autumn leaves.

A bumblebee with polka dot dreams,
Buzzes past with funny schemes.
"Catch a smile, it's worth the chase!"
In this pursuit, we find our place.

Silly hats and pie on face,
Together in this joyful race.
Laughter loops in endless trails,
As we unveil life's funny tales.

Searching high and searching low,
In every corner, let happiness flow.
The greatest treasure that we acquire,
Are the smiles that never tire.

Revelry in Reflection

Mirrors giggling, showing grace,
We catch ourselves in a silly chase.
Dancing shadows, twirling light,
In our flaws, we find delight.

Reflections crack and shimmer bright,
Each wrinkle tells of sheer delight.
A comical wink, a playful pose,
In this mirth, our spirit grows.

With popcorn clouds and cozy nights,
We wrap our hearts in laughter's sights.
In fragile moments, strength is found,
In the absurd, joy's profound.

So toast to life with silly cheers,
Embrace the quirks, dismiss the fears.
For in this dance of ups and downs,
We weave the fabric of life's crowns.

Breezy Paths of Discovery

On a path of twists and turns,
Life's a game with lots to learn.
With each stumble, we find our way,
A giggle at the mess we play.

Puzzles pop up, some are wild,
We dance like an awkward child.
Chasing shadows, winking bright,
In this silly, joyous plight.

With maps drawn in crayon hues,
We chase the dreams and chase our blues.
Every folly leads to gold,
In laughter, our hearts unfold.

So let's prance with glee and grace,
In the jester's warm embrace.
For every twist along this road,
Is just a jest in a funny code.

The Art of Comedic Contemplation

In moments deep with furrowed brow,
We find the funny, strike a vow.
Tickle thoughts like gentle breeze,
In pondering, let giggles tease.

Witty whims and quirky signs,
In curious hearts, wisdom shines.
A thought can tickle, make you grin,
Like irony wrapped in a spin.

Philosophers with laughter's spark,
Chase ideas from dawn till dark.
Jokes and jests are ways to cope,
With a wink, we fuel our hope.

So muse with whimsy, take a chance,
Let your mind do a silly dance.
For every ponder, comedically spun,
Brings joy in the race that's never done.

The Humor of Seeking

On a quest for gems so rare,
We wear our fumbles, "Aren't we fair?"
Silly signs and clues amass,
Through muddled paths, we all just pass.

Frogs in bow ties, rabbits in hats,
We tiptoe forth, where laughter pats.
Every misstep is a surprise,
Sending grins to the clear blue skies.

With every question, we entice,
What's beyond isn't so precise.
Yet here we are, hearts in full bloom,
Finding joy in every room.

So chase the moon with playful cheer,
Embrace the odd, it's all sincere.
For in the chase, we truly find,
It's funny how we're intertwined.

Glee in the Great Unknown

In vast horizons, we do roam,
The unknown whispers, "Welcome home!"
With every step, a jest we weave,
The world at large, it makes us leave.

Clouds in shapes of ice cream cones,
And laughter ringing through our bones.
We take our time, a joyful jest,
In grand adventures, we feel blessed.

With rollicking hearts and quirky dreams,
We craft our stories with giggling seams.
In every journey, we meet delight,
Glee ignites the dark of night.

So here we venture, hand in hand,
Among the wonders, false and grand.
In the dance of life, we find our flow,
Embracing all, as we laugh and grow.

The Jester's Path

In a world that spins quite round,
A jester dances, joy unbound.
With every step, a silly twirl,
He tickles fate, gives life a whirl.

With painted face and wild delight,
He shares his tricks both day and night.
Each merry twist, a lesson shared,
In laughter's grip, all burdens bared.

Through gardens green and skies so blue,
He juggles dreams; they come true too.
In foolishness, there's wisdom found,
As giggles echo all around.

So travel on, oh merry fool,
In jest, we find a hidden jewel.
With smiles and puns, we weave our tale,
And ride the waves of life's grand gale.

Echoes of Laughter

In shadows deep, a cackle rises,
A whisper floats with sweet surprises.
What rumbles forth but hearty cheer,
And echoes back, just lend an ear.

The clouds may loom and frowns may glare,
Yet giggles bounce through the thick air.
Footfalls light, like tickled toes,
We dance through life, as laughter flows.

A jumbled thought, a silly face,
In quirks and quirks, we find our place.
They say the world is filled with gloom,
But chase the dark; it finds no room.

So let the chuckles fill our hearts,
In every turn, delight imparts.
The echoes swirl, a joyful ring,
And life unveils its playful swing.

The Quest for a Grin

With curious eyes, we roam the street,
Chasing giggles on our feet.
What treasures lie in laughter's bloom,
From silly hats to fun costumes?

We seek a grin in crowded halls,
Where nonsense reigns and freedom calls.
Each hearty laugh, a golden find,
In silly rhymes, our hearts unwind.

Through every joke and playful jest,
We search for joy; we seek the best.
In burdens light, we'll surely win,
For happiness is never thin.

So off we go, embrace the fun,
With every laugh, we're never done.
In every quest, let chuckles sing,
And let our spirits take to wing.

Curious Heartbeats

In the realm of giggles bright,
Curious hearts take daring flight.
With every ponder, every scheme,
We chase the joy, a wild dream.

What tickles minds and sparks delight,
Are moments shared both day and night.
With laughter soft and chuckles loud,
We find our kind, our silly crowd.

Through paths of whimsy, we will roam,
In every chuckle, we feel at home.
So let the joy in each heartbeat soar,
And paint the world with fun galore.

A curious jest, a playful tease,
In life's grand play, we take our ease.
Each laugh we share, a bond we glean,
And in our hearts, forever sheen.

www.ingramcontent.com/pod-product-compliance
Lightning Source LLC
Chambersburg PA
CBHW072148200426
43209CB00051B/846